12 PEACHTREE

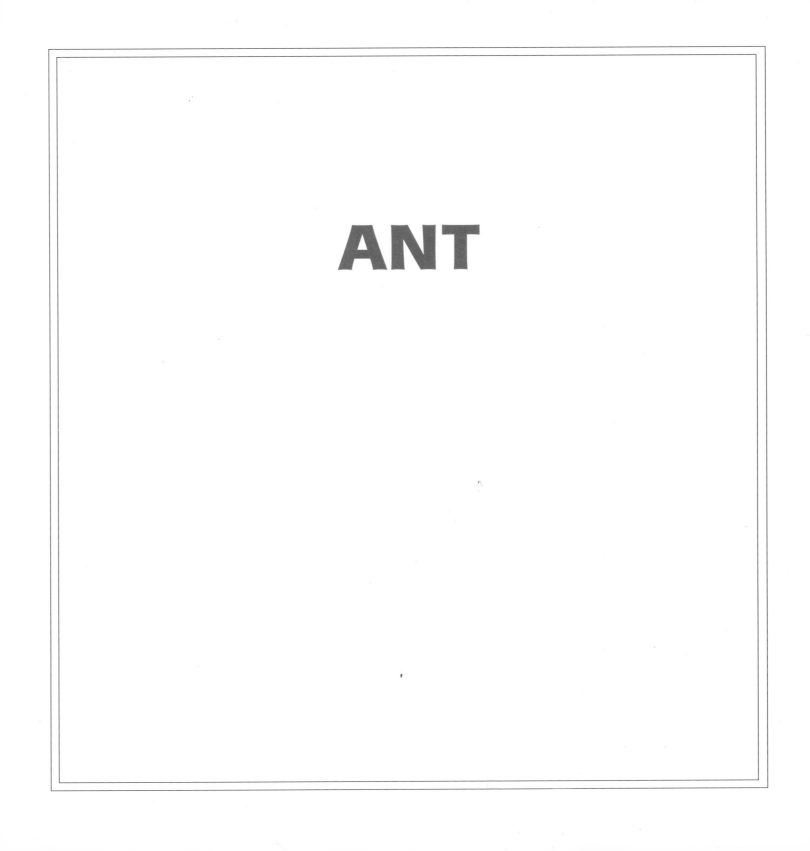

ANT

LIVING THINGS

ANT

Rebecca Stefoff

BENCHMARK BOOKS

MARSHALL CAVENDISH
NEW YORK

Benchmark Books
Marshall Cavendish Corporation
99 White Plains Road
Tarrytown, New York 10591-9001

Illustrations by Lisa Bonforte

Library of Congress Cataloging-in-Publication Data
Stefoff, Rebecca, date.
Ant / by Rebecca Stefoff.
p.   cm. — (Living things)
Includes index.
Summary: Examines the physical characteristics, life cycle,
and natural habitat of various types of ants.
ISBN 0-7614-0447-3 (lib. bdg.)
1 Ants—Juvenile literature. [1. Ants.]
I.Title. II. Series: Stefoff, Rebecca, date.   Living things.
QL568.F7S77   1998   595.79'6—dc21   97-9132   CIP   AC

Photo research by Ellen Barrett Dudley

Cover photo: *Animals Animals*, Raymond A. Mendez

The photographs in this book are used by permission and through the courtesy of:
The National Audubon Society Collection/Photo Researchers, Inc.: L. West, 2;
Gary Retherford, 7, 16 (left), 22-23; Len Rue Jr., 8 (left); Jerome Wexler, 8 (right);
Leonard Lee Rue, 9; J.H. Robinson, 10, 11; Leonide Principe, 13 (top); Rudolph
Freund, 13 (bottom); S.J. Krasemann, 14 (top); John Dommers, 14 (bottom);
John Serrao, 15; Gregory G. Dimijian, 18 (right), 19; Varin/Jacana, 26-27.
Peter Arnold, Inc.: Hans Pfletschinger, 6-7, 12 (left), 12-13, 24, 25; Kevin Schafer,
17 (top); S.J. Krasemann, 17 (bottom). *Animals Animals*: Philip K. Sharpe, 16-17;
K.G. Preston-Mafham, 18 (left); Donald Specker, 20; Mantis Wildlife Films,
Oxford Scientific Films, 21; Richard K. La Val, 32.

Printed in the United States of America

1   3   5   6   4   2

For my industrious pal Suzanne

red ants

black ant, Costa Rica

Ants.

They're everywhere. You can see ants in almost any part of the world.

But you hardly ever see just one ant. If you see an ant, you will probably find lots of other ants nearby.

7

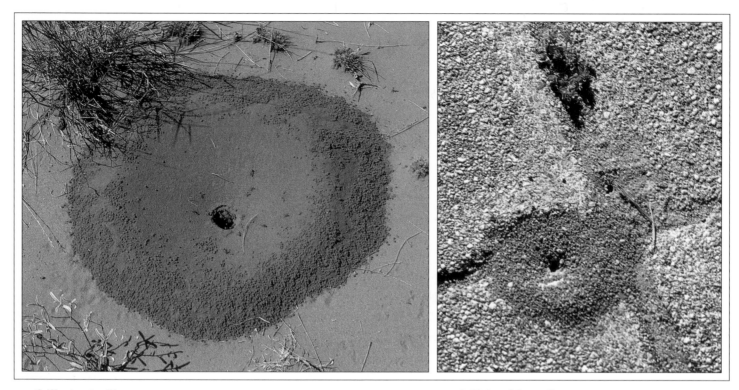

anthill, Australia

anthill in sidewalk

Ants live and work together in busy, crowded groups called colonies. Most colonies are in tunnels under the ground. The ants carry dirt out of the tunnels to make a pile. We call these piles anthills.

When you see an anthill in a sidewalk crack, you know there is a city of ants under the sidewalk.

Some anthills are huge and filled with tunnels. An ant colony has lived under this tree for years. Each year the ants dig new tunnels and make the anthill a little bigger.

anthill, East Africa

Every ant has two long, waving stalks on its head. These are its antennae. They are like a nose and fingers all in one.

The antennae tell the ant what is going on around it. They help it find food and then find its way back to its colony.

These two ants are "talking" by rubbing their antennae together. The big ant is the queen. She is the mother of all the ants in the colony. The little ant is a worker. Workers take care of the queen's eggs and bring food to the colony.

Ants do all kinds of things together. They pass pieces of food to each another. Sometimes they even carry each other around.

Some jobs are too big for one ant. That's when ants team up. A bunch of little ants working together can carry a big dead bug. It will make a fine meal for the colony.

Ants take a shortcut between tree branches. Some of them hold one another's legs to make a bridge. Others can walk across the bridge to the new branch.

ants carrying dead stick insect, Brazil

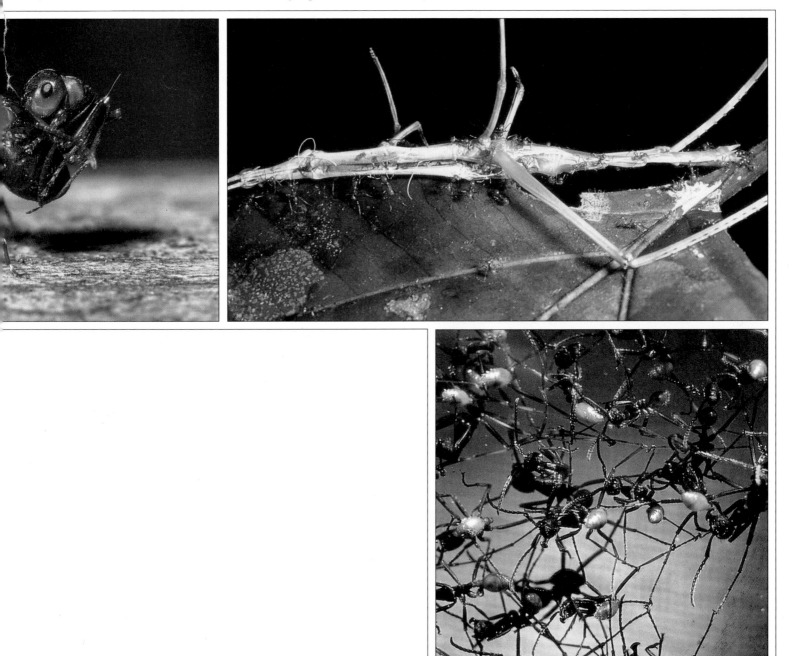

ant bridge, Panama

Carpenter ants live in wood. A pile of yellow sawdust on a log means that carpenter ants are busy inside, chewing new tunnels.

Deep in the log, the queen's eggs are turning into larvae. When the larvae hatch from their cocoons, they look like little worms. Later the larvae will turn into ants and pour out of the log.

Leafcutter ants live in Central and South America. Some people call them parasol ants. Do you know why?

The ants chew off pieces of leaves and

carry them back to their tunnels.
They march with the leaves held
over their heads like little sun-
shades, or parasols.

The ants don't eat the leaves.
They chew them into a paste. A
yellow fungus grows on the paste,
and the ants eat the fungus.

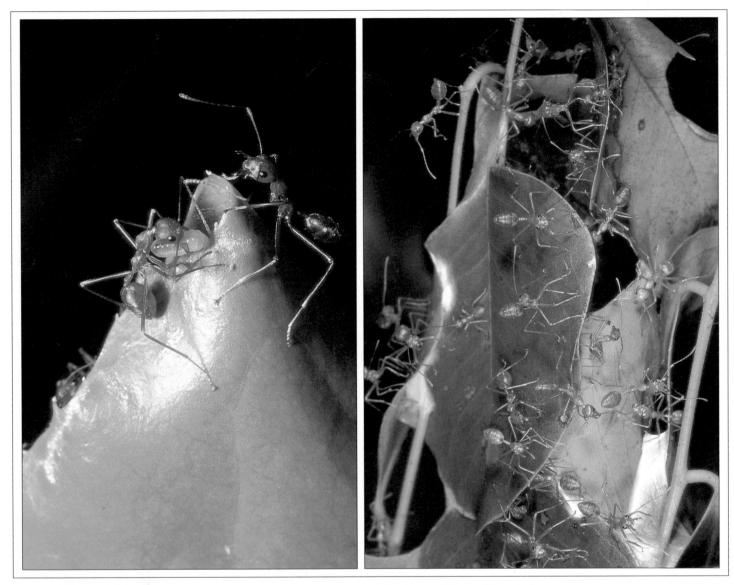

weaver ants with larva

white larval thread binds leaves

Weaver ants live in trees in southern Asia and on Pacific islands. They make nests by fastening leaves together with sticky silk thread. The thread comes from the young ants, or larvae. Older ants hold the larvae that spin the thread.

Teams of ants join together into chains to bend the big, stiff leaves.

nest making, Australia

farmer ants with aphids, New York

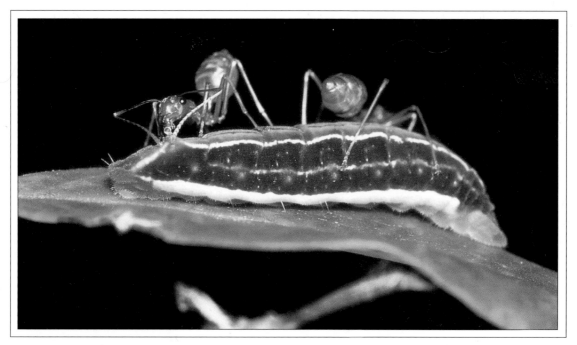

ants "milking" caterpillar

Some ants eat juices that come from inside other insects. They take care of these insects and "milk" them for their juice, like a farmer milks a herd of cows.

The little green bugs are plant eaters called aphids. The ants tending them are called farmer ants.

Army ants live in tropical jungles. They march from place to place, eating plants and insects as they go. They climb right over logs and rocks and even houses.

A colony of army ants on the march covers the ground like a moving, munching carpet. Some colonies are as wide as a street and as long as a city block.

army ants, Costa Rica

A lot of little ants working together can beat one big black beetle. When it comes to teamwork, ants are experts.

Can you pick up your mother and carry her over your head? You could if you were an ant. Ants are very strong. They can carry things that weigh a lot more then they do. It takes only two ants to lift this fat caterpillar.

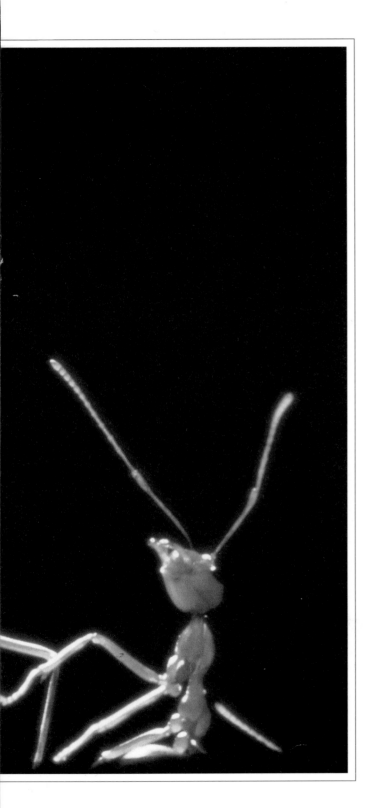

Ants live in colonies that
are like cities. They help one
another, and they work together
on big jobs.
 I think ants are a lot like us.
 Do you?

A QUICK LOOK AT THE ANT

Ants belong to the large group of living things called insects. Ants have lived on earth for more than 100 million years. Scientists know of about nine thousand different kinds, or species, of ants. They think that thousands of other species are still to be identified. Ants are found everywhere in the world except in the polar regions. They are most numerous in the tropics, where the greatest variety of species is found.

Here are five kinds of ants, along with their scientific names and a few key facts. You'll also get a look inside an anthill.

LITTLE BLACK ANT

Monomorium minimum
(mah noh MOH ree um MIH nih mum)
Measures 1/16 inch (1.6 mm). Found throughout North America except in Pacific Northwest. One of the most common ants in houses. Also lives on forest edges.

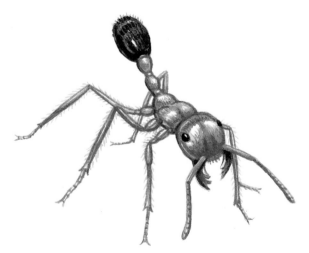

FIRE ANT

Solenopsis geminata
(soh leh NOP sis jeh mih NAY tuh)
Measures 1/16 to 1/4 inch (1.6–6.4 mm). Found in Florida and along Gulf of Mexico coast, north to British Columbia. Originally from South America, fire ants have become agricultural pests in the southeastern United States. Their bite is painful.

BIG-HEADED ANT
Pheidole Megacephala
(fay DOH leh meh gah SEH fah luh)
Measures 1/16 to 1/8 inch (1.6–3 mm).
Head is bigger than body. Lives in small
colonies in Florida fields and gardens.
Eats seeds and grain.

HONEY ANT
Prenolepsis imparis
(preh noh LEP sis IM pah ris)
Measures 1/16 to 1/8 inch (1.6–3 mm).
Lives in shady, damp soil from Wisconsin
and Ontario south to Florida, west to the
Pacific. Forages at night for flower nectar,
dead insects, and worms.

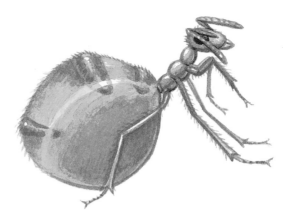

BLACK CARPENTER ANT *Camponatus pennsylvanicus*
(cam poh NAY tus pen sil VAY nih cus)
Measures 1/4 to 1/2 inch
(6.4–12.7 mm).
Lives in dead trees, logs,
and the wood of houses
from Quebec, Canada,
south to Florida.
Can give sharp bite.

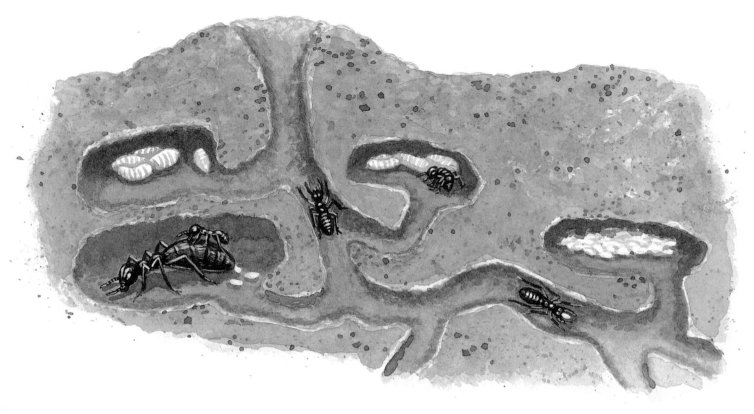

Taking Care of the Ant

Most people worry more about getting rid of ants than about protecting them. Are ants pests? They damage crops and property, but they do more good than harm. By tunneling through the earth, ants break up the soil and make it easier for plants to grow. They are also an important part of the earth's "clean-up crew," which eats dead and decaying plants and animals.

Find Out More

Bix, Cynthia Overbeck. *Ants*. Minneapolis: Lerner Publications, 1982.

Butterworth, Christine. *Ants*. Morristown, N.J.: Silver Burdett, 1988.

Demuth, Patricia. *Those Amazing Ants*. New York: Macmillan, 1994.

Dorros, Arthur. *Ant Cities*. New York: Harper & Row, 1987.

Fischer-Nagel, Heiderose. *An Ant Colony*. Minneapolis: Carolrhoda Books, 1989.

O'Toole, Christopher. *Discovering Ants*. New York: Bookwright Press, 1986.

Patent, Dorothy Hinshaw. *Looking at Ants*. New York: Holiday House, 1989.

Sabin, Francene. *Amazing World of Ants*. Mahwah, N.J.: Troll, 1982.

Index

Rebecca Stefoff has published many books for young readers. Science and environmental issues are among her favorite subjects. She lives in Oregon and enjoys observing the natural world while hiking, camping, and scuba diving.

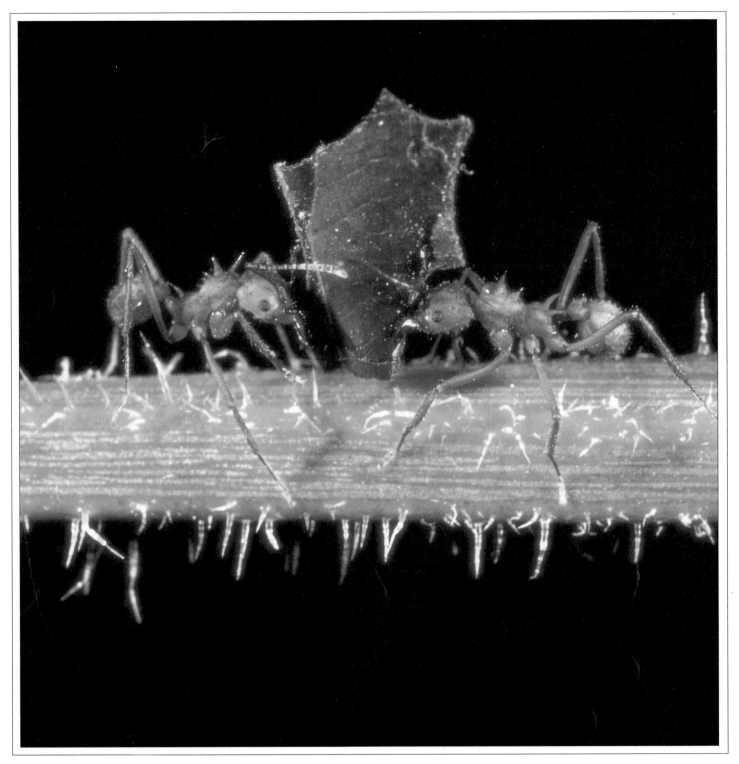

leaf cutter ants, Costa Rica